MW00873644

Spring Woodland Wildflowers in the Midwest

A Pocket Guide

Tess Park

Parkwood Publishing, Carmel, IN

Contents

Dedication

To all who wish to stay young at heart, whether young in years or not, especially my mother, who was ninety-two in May. This guide is for all, who like my husband, Jay, son, John, and I, love to spend time in the woods to see what wonders nature has to offer. We want to know the names of all the things we see there because as we get to know them, they are like meeting old friends again and bring us joy.

The poem on the following page was written by my Mom and published with permission.

The Wonder of Spring

By Wilma Lee Kincade Jansen Pierce

Snowdrops and aconites push through
   winter's frozen soil, liberating
   themselves to beautify the earth.

Spring's fragile hands bring warmth
   with no toil, loosening fingers of
   winter as she shows her true worth.

Beauties and Anemones soon show their
   faces, making way for Trout Lilies
   and Trilliums to decorate the woods.

All now are splendorous as they sway
   with the breezes, and the awakening
   of lower canopies add to the mood.

With the smell of fresh grasses and
   scallion, Daffodils and Wood Poppies
   in turn unfold.

The loveliness of the blossoms' sweet
   yellow brilliance, turns the yard
   golden, pleasing senses untold.

So hurry up, wildflowers! We wait your
   sweet presence, of Green Dragons,
   Jacks, and fern's laces.

Blessed sunshine, so welcome, you
   bring us delight and wonder and
   awe in all places.

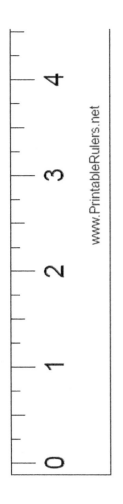

0   1   2   3   4

www.PrintableRulers.net

To scale ruler in inches divided into 1/4" to measure flower parts. This ruler is only valid for the printed version and not for the digital version.

Introduction

Spring wildflowers are the best reason to shake off winter's inactivity and go for a walk in the woods. Most are perennial and some are ephemeral perennials which are short-lived wildflowers that grow, bloom, pollinate and produce seeds in spring then die back by summer as the deciduous tree leaves above emerge and result in deep shade in the woods. Some spring wildflowers' foliage and seeds persist until fall. Most woodland plants prefer a moist, high organic matter in the soil and full to partial shade. The show usually lasts for 5-6 weeks, so every few days holds a different surprise, enticing us to explore often to enjoy nature's surprises.

How to Use this Guide

"A picture is worth a thousand words" is an old saying that comes to mind in creating this quick pocket guide. My goal is to include a photograph, my own, that includes the flower and foliage, as the plant allows, and if the plant is too tall, a photograph of each which occurs in the spring. In creating this small pocket guide, the intention is to provide a very brief description of the flower and plant size for a proper perspective and quick identification. Extreme close-up photographs sometimes give a wrong impression about flower size when first learning to identify, so a figure in inches or fractions of inches is helpful for initial ID. The flowers are arranged by color. Some change color as they age or can occur in white and a pastel color. Also arranged and noted is when

Pages 15 - 65   whites, pastel pinks or blues.

Pages 66 - 78 yellows, intense and sunny.

Pages 79 - 88   maroon, deep red-brown

Pages 89 - 90 deep purples.

they appear in early, mid, or late Spring. This is a layman's guide, so it does not go into scientific botanical descriptions. References in the back will take you to more scientific botanical detail.

CAUTION: I've included two especially poisonous plants that you need to know for safety. Many plants have been medicinal in ancient times because they contain active chemicals. Take photos and leave the plants where they know how to grow.

Notes of favorite wildflower places and dates:
(for print version only. If E-book, be sure to create a digital quick note on your phone)

_____

_____

_____

_____

_____

_____

_____

_____

_____

_____

_____

_____

_____

** Poison Hemlock *Conium maculatum* **

This is a plant to know but **not touch**. The juices of this plant are poisonous and **kills by causing respiratory arrest and heart failure**. It is toxic to humans and animals. It is one of the deadliest plants in North America and can be fatal if just a small amount is ingested. It is often confused with Queen Anne's Lace or other plants in the carrot family. Many people walk past this species without even realizing what it is. It was introduced in the 1800's and is now found in nearly every part of North America. Tiny white flowers form umbrella-shaped clusters. Fern-like compound leaves taper to a point. Stems with purple splotches can grow 2 - 10' tall. It is a biennial which only flowers it's second season. It seeds and spreads easily. Infestations can be seen along roadsides almost everywhere when in bloom. It invades at field edges, ditches, and meadows, preferring shaded areas with moist soil.

** CAUTION: Poison Hemlock **

Poison Ivy *Toxicodendron radicans*

"Leaves of three, let it be" is a rule to follow in the outdoors. Identify and avoid this poisonous plant. In early spring, it emerges with a reddish color before the mature leaves turn green. It can appear as a groundcover up to 3' tall or a

** CAUTION: Poison Ivy **

woody vine with roots that can cling to the surface climbing up trees, buildings, or poles up to 60' tall. The leaves are comprised of three 2-1/2" x 4" leaflets. The middle leaflet has 2 "thumbs," the outer leaflets have outer "thumbs." Two other sayings to remember this plant are: "Berries of white, run in fright" and "Hairy vine, no friend of mine." If any part of the plant is exposed to skin, it will create an itchy rash and blisters. DO NOT BURN Poison Ivy because it can cause a severe breathing problem if the smoke is inhaled. The oily poisonous substance, urushiol, can also be transferred to skin for years by gardening implements or other objects that have come in contact with the plant, such as shovels, rakes, backpacks and hair coats of dogs. Try to remove the oily urushiol within an hour or two of contact with skin by washing vigorously with dish detergent as if you were trying to remove used motor oil. Wash multiple times without rubbing too hard and <u>do not</u> use any abrasive cloth or brush. It's the detergent that will remove the urushiol oil with gentle yet thorough rubbing.

Please study the parts of a flower.

Free illustration **www.pinterest.com/wonderwildlife/**

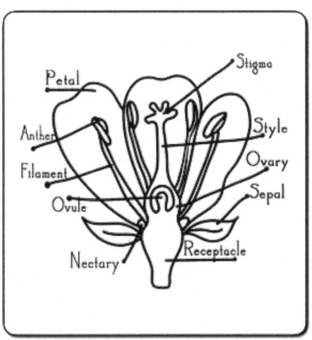

Wonderweirded Botany Lab

Study Card

wonderweirded-wildlife.com

Harbinger of Spring
Erigenia bulbosa

Very early, this tiny first spring flower is often overlooked, as it is only 3 - 4" tall. The highly dissected leaves look like the tops of carrots. Also called **Pepper & Salt,** because the dark red anthers sit atop the tiny white petals. After the bloom, the delicate foliage persists in the background, gathering energy in its tiny corm as the other spring wildflowers take the stage.

Snow Trillium
Trillium nivale

A very early perennial often found while snow is on the ground, it is only 2 - 5" tall on one stem with a cluster of 3 oval leaves (bracts). In the center is a short pedicle and flower that has 3 white oval petals nearly 1" long and 3 shorter green sepals. The anthers are yellow. It reproduces mainly by rhizomes. It is rare and usually found on dry bluffs or steep slopes that provide a loamy soil, thin leaf layer with no competition.

Sharp-lobed Hepatica
Hepatica nobilis acuta

Very early. Small, 3/4" lavender to white blooms with 6 - 8 petals emerge before the foliage unfurls to replace the evergreen foliage of the prior year which is usually buried under the leaves. Later spring, the foliage emerges under the flowers and eventually deepens its mottling. It is a small 6" perennial with 3 lobes to the 2" leaves which persist evergreen. Previous year foliage at the base. There is also a round leaf form.

Bloodroot
Sanguinaria canadensis

Early. Single white flowers, 1 - 2" diameter with 8 - 12 petals arranged in a circle that open when sunny. Leaves are a 4 - 10" single, multi-lobed leaf which looks like a musical instrument called a lyre and persist throughout the growing season. It is named for the red sap of its rhizome as in the Latin word sanguinaria, which means bleeding.

Spring Beauty
Claytonia virginica

Early ephemeral, lasting to mid-season. Leaves narrowly lance-shaped to 3" long, on a 3 - 6" tall plant. Flowers are white or pale pink and pink striped, 1/2" wide, with 5 petals. It is one of the most common spring wildflowers in the woods and can be seen covering lawns that have not been treated with herbicides.

Twinleaf *Jeffersonia diphylla*

Mid-spring. Twinleaf grows 6 to 10" tall, has one white flower atop a leafless stalk about 1" wide with eight petals and four sepals. The flowers last only about 24 hours so it is rare to find it in bloom. It is extremely slow to multiply. It has clump-forming, long-stemmed, blue to green basal leaves (to 6") which are deeply divided into two lobes that give the appearance of being two separate leaves, thus Twinleaf. The botanical Latin name honors Thomas Jefferson, the 3rd president of the USA.

Trout Lily, White
Erythronium albidum

Mid-spring ephemeral. Leaves are 4 - 6" long elliptical and mottled with brown splotches, resembling a trout fish. Foliage and size similar to yellow trout lily (pg. 67) but with white flowers. Indiana is one of the few states in which both yellow and white trout lilies can be found together, although moisture preferences are slightly different.

Dutchman's Breeches
Dicentra cucullaria

Mid-spring, up to 8" tall, highly dissected leaves with 3/4" white flowers with two pointed spurs having 2 white outer petals and 2 inner petals that are pale yellow. Four or more flowers are alternately suspended from a short stalk above the leaves resembling pants hanging upside down. The foliage is similar to squirrel corn but usually blooms slightly earlier, although both can be seen together.

Squirrel Corn
Dicentra canadensis

Mid-spring. Each plant is around 6" tall, leaves highly dissected, 3/4" white flowers are heart-shaped with two rounded spurs at the bottom and 4 - 6 flowers stand above the foliage on a short stalk. It flowers slightly later than Dutchman's breeches, is less common, and resembles flowers of Old Fashioned Bleeding Heart. Squirrel corn is named for the yellow corm from which it sprouts.

False Rue Anemone
Isopyrum biternatum

Mid-spring ephemeral with 3/4" white, single flowers on stems above the delicate, short foliage 4 - 8" tall with compound leaves. It forms large colonies rather than single clumps. There are five letters in false and five petal-like sepals to this flower, so that is an easy way to remember because it is often confused with Rue Anemone, which blooms at the same time but has slightly different characteristics.

Rue Anemone
Thalictrum thalictroides

Mid-spring. On a short stem, flowers are 3/4" white to pastel pinkish-lavender petal-like sepals which give them a longer bloom time. It often has 6 - 10 sepals instead of five of False Rue Anemone. The leaflets are not deeply incised on the compound leaves. Grows in single clumps, 6 - 8" tall, rather than colonies, and prefers wooded slopes or sites with good drainage.

Spring Cress
Cardamine bulbosa

Mid-spring. With a cluster of small flowers at the top, each flower has 4 rounded petals, about 1/2" across at the end of a 1 - 2' tall, slender, erect stem, not usually branched. Flowers may be fragrant and last for three weeks. Alternate leaves are very widely spaced along the stem, about 1" x 1-1/4" oval,

with smooth or wavy margins. Basal leaves are about 1" x 2", oval or kidney-shaped, hairless, with a wavy edge (see photo next page) and may be gone by flowering time. It reproduces by seed or tubers.

Cutleaf Toothwort
Cardamine concatenata
aka: *Dentaria laciniata*

Mid-spring. Each plant is 5 - 10" tall with a whorl of 3 deeply dissected leaves topped by a cluster of pink to white 4-petaled flowers which are 1/2" long. The flowers, in sun, open to a white four-pointed star. Fragrant flowers bloom for about two weeks. The plant lives in colonies spreading by rhizomes and seeds. It owes its name to the tooth-like appearance of its rhizome.

Striped Cream Violet
Viola striata

Mid-spring. Small, creamy white five petal flowers, about 3/4" across, with a purple veined lower petal that rises from a leafy stem. Grows 6 - 12" tall. Dark green, heart-shaped leaves with deeply cut stipules can form a thick ground cover. It prefers moist, rich woods, bottomlands, and stream banks. There are nine species of white violet, some with leafless stems, so please refer to scientific references for proper ID.

Confederate Violet
Viola sororia priceana

Mid-spring. See **Common Blue Violet** for description. This violet is a subspecies and the flower sits on top of a leafless stem above heart shaped, serrated edge leaves. The flower has numerous violet stripes going through the white petals which gives it a gray appearance, the color of Confederate Soldier Uniforms.

Dwarf Crested Iris

Iris cristata

A mid-spring perennial only 3 - 6" tall. It's pale blue to lavender iris flowers have gold crests on the falls. Flowers are on very short stems sprouting out of branching rhizomes. It spreads quickly and can form dense colonies. It can be found on rocky, wooded slopes, on bluffs and along streams. It will be growing in rich organic, medium moisture, well-drained soils in full to part shade. When it is found in full sun it will be in a seep that keeps the soil consistently moist but well-drained.

Large-flowered Trillium
Trillium grandiflorum

Mid-spring. Leaves, petals, and sepals all come in threes. The stem is unbranched and rises up 12 - 18" tall topped by 3 veined, green 3 - 6" oval leaves. From the center grows a single flower on an upright, arching stalk 2 - 3" tall. Each flower 2 - 3" diameter has 3 wavy white petals and 3 small green sepals. Flowers turn pink with age. Seeds are disbursed by ants. Foliage will usually die to the ground by late summer, particularly if soils are dry.

Wild Blue Phlox
Phlox divaricata

Mid-late spring. **Woodland Phlox** or **Sweet William** because of the sweet aromatic fragrance. It is a semi-evergreen, spreading wildflower 9 - 12" tall, which creates mats of abundant, open clusters of flowers in shades of lilac, rose or blue radiating out from the tip of the stem. The stems are sticky and hairy, and the leaves are opposite.

Drooping Trillium
Trillium flexipes

Mid-spring. Single white flower up to 2" wide with 3 petals & 3 sepals hangs down from a peduncle stem about 2" long, thus drooping. *The anthers are pale and considerably longer than the filaments, creating a shorter stamen that is about half the length of the pistil and does not reach the stigma.* Leaves are oval to 6" long, smooth and hairless. The 1 - 2' tall plants live in small colonies, and are spread by rhizomes. The fruit is a single berry about 1-1/4" long, 6-sided with distinct angles and ripens from green to maroon.

** Nodding Trillium *Trillium cernuum*

Almost identical to the Drooping Trillium, however, the *dark anthers are on a longer filament creating a longer stamen that nearly reaches the length of the pistil at the stigma. The pistil (female part) consists of the stigma, style, and ovary which contains the ovules. The stamen (male parts) consist of the filament and the anther, which holds the pollen.*

That, my friends, is the subtle difference between the two, drooping vs. nodding trilliums. Also, *T. cernuum* (Nodding), in Indiana, is only found near Lake Michigan and is a smaller plant than *T. flexipes* (Drooping).

Virginia Bluebells
Mertensia virginica

Mid-spring. Bell-shaped flowers about 1" long, emerge pink and gradually turn light lavender-

blue as they mature. They prefer moisture. Plants are 1 - 2' tall with large smooth, alternate, oval, bluish-green leaves, up to 7" long. Over time they form large colonies. Foliage dies back by mid-summer as the plant goes dormant. Hummingbirds and bumblebees will often be seen visiting these flowers. Only the largest bees can push their way up the tube.

Rare pink form of Mertensia virginica

Blue-Eyed Mary *Collinsia verna*

Mid-late spring. This winter annual is up to 12" tall. The 3/4" flowers, somewhat similar to violets, have upper white lips and lower blue

lips, slightly cleft. Several flowers sit at the top of the stem, each on their own pedicle and last about 3 weeks. It has a central, unbranched stem with 3/4" x 2" opposite leaves. The lower leaves are oval and have a few blunt teeth on the margins. The upper leaves are thinner and smooth along their margins. It spreads by reseeding.

Navel Corn Salad   *Valerianella umbilicata*

Late. An annual wildflower that is 1 - 2' tall. It begins with a rosette of basal leaves 3/4" x 2-1/2" then shoots up a central stem

where the leaves are opposite and up to 1" x 3" oblong. The terminal stem divides in two and holds the cluster of tiny 1/8" white to pink flowers. The 5 petals fuse to form a corolla (funnel). When tiny seeds form they are indented like a navel. It prefers dappled sun and consistently moist, sandy, organic matter soil near stream flood planes. Uncommon.

Field Pussytoes
Antennaria neglecta

Late. Flower clusters are white, cottony tufts 1/4" spheres rising 8 - 12" above basal leaves which form a rosette. Each leaf is about 1/2" x 2", with a tapered, pointed tip. Each flowering stalk has tiny alternate leaves. Found at the woods edge where there is more sun, good drainage, and the soil is less fertile. Pussytoes are a host plant for caterpillars of the American Painted Lady butterfly.

Star Chickweed   *Stellaria pubera*

Late spring flowering plants grow 6 - 12" tall, unbranched with opposite leaves up to 1-1/4" x 3" oblong. The upper surface of these leaves is medium to dark green, slightly hairy and smooth margins. Tiny white flowers 1/2" diameter with 5 petals so deeply cleft they look like 10 petals. The bloom lasts nearly a month.

It has a taproot with slender fibrous roots. Small colonies of plants are occasionally formed. It is but a tiny star in the Spring woodland flower show.

White Baneberry   *Actaea pachypoda*

Late. The spherical clusters of tiny white flowers appear above the foliage. The plant has tall, 1 - 3' branched stems that have 2 to 3 large compound leaves. Leaflets are deeply toothed creating a feathery appearance. Also called **Doll's Eyes** for the shiny white fruit that appears in late summer which resembles the china eyes used to make antique dolls.

This is what the "doll's eyes" look like in late summer as the foliage is declining.

Red Baneberry *Actaea rubra*

Late. The plant is 1 - 3' tall and rarely branched. Very similar to White Baneberry, except the berries are glossy red (rarely white) and stalks more slender. Leaves are twice compound with 3 or 5 leaflets in each group. Leaflets are up to 2" x 2" with sharp coarse teeth, rounded base, and pointed tip.

Violet Wood Sorrel
Oxalis violacea

A late perennial, 6" tall with pink to lavender flowers with 5 petals and pale throats containing yellow anthers on leafless stalks. The leaf stems grow from the bulb as well and 1" leaves look like purple-tinted clover with 3 heart-shaped leaves. It can spread by runners from the bulbs to create large colonies.

Jack-in-the-Pulpit
Arisaema triphyllum

Late. Plants are 8 - 18" tall, have one to two large, glossy leaves, divided into 3 leaflets that stand on their stems. The blossom occurs on a separate stalk, is white or purple striped, and bends over to hide a green club-like spadix (Jack).

Later in spring, a cluster of green berries turn red and last until early summer, then are eaten by Wood Thrush and Wild Turkey.

Green Dragon
Arisaema dracontium

Late. Similar to Jack-in-the-pulpit, but it has a compound leaf with several oblong leaflets (7 -15) with an umbrella shape on a single stem. The flower, on a separate stem, has a small hood and a long, green spadix that tapers. It is dormant in the summer, after producing red berries. It is 1 - 3' tall and 12 - 18" wide. It is toxic, containing calcium oxalate.

Mayapple
Podophyllum peltatum

Late spring. Grows in colonies 1 to 1-1/2' tall. Deeply incised umbrella-like leaves are about 1' wide. White flowers are found in the junction of the leaf stalks and stem. Fruit is round, greenish yellow, about 1-1/2" to 2." The ripened fruit is edible but the rest of the plant is poisonous. It can take about 7 years from seedling to fruit.

Solomon's Seal
Polygonatum biflorum

A late spring plant that grows in a slight arc 2 - 3' tall, alternate leaves attached to a central stem. Smooth, oval, pointed leaves 2" x 5 - 6." White bell flowers hide under the stem and hang down, later forming berries that ripen to purple and are eaten by birds. A scar on the rhizome said to look like the seal of King Solomon.

False Solomon's Seal
Maianthemum racemosum

Late. Perennial grows 2 - 3' tall, slowly spreads by rhizomes, often forming large colonies. Unbranched, gracefully arching stems of alternate, oval, pointed, light green leaves with parallel veins. Tiny, fragrant, white flowers at the stem end as a terminal plume, turn into green berries that are red in summer and eaten by wildlife.

Sweet Cicely
Osmorhiza longistylis

Late. Also called Sweet Anise because its fragrant anise scented roots, leaves, and stems remind one of licorice candy. Tiny white flower clusters grow on branched stems 1 - 3' tall. Fern-like leaves, up to 12", are broad, triple compound, slightly toothed, with compound flat clusters of tiny, white flowers. Each flower cluster has 8 - 16 tiny flowers and up to 5 compound clusters. Each 1/8" flower has 5 white petals and stamens with 2 white styles that are longer than the petals. It prefers rich,

moist woods, wooded slopes, and ravines.

Shooting Star
Dodecatheon meadia

Late. Pink or white flowers on a leafless stalk 6 - 20" tall emerging from bright green basal leaf cluster. Blossoms look like darts with five petals swept back, dangling from the tall stems. Two colorful bands of deep purple and golden

yellow circle the base of each flower. Leaves are oblong, 2" x 6" with smooth edges and greyish green in color.

Putty Root Orchid
Aplectrum hyemale

Late. Flowers 3/4" - 1" are pale greenish yellow, showing maroon at the tips, arranged in a sparse raceme. They have 3 sepals, 3 petals, stamen, and pistol. Each raceme contains 8 - 16 flowers on a 6 - 20" tall stalk. Blooms last 2 - 3 weeks. The single basal leaf develops in the fall, lasts through winter until it flowers in late spring. This green basal leaf is 1" - 3" by 3-1/2" - 8", oval with smooth margins, has fine white parallel veins, and lays nearly flat on the ground. These basal leaves turn yellow and disappear in the summer. Underground, the corms are connected by rhizomes and colonize.

Leaves have fine white lines. Last year's stems hold seedpods.

Goldenseal
Hydrastis canadensis

Mid to late flowering perennial, it grows up to 15" tall with 8 to 10" wrinkled maple-like leaves when young, then expands and looses it's wrinkles later in the season. The blossom has no petals, the sepals fall off, and the flower consists of many white stamens and about 10 pistils in the center. By late summer, this turns into a cluster of red berries. The plant expands via it's yellow rhizomes (thus its name) and seeds. It can be found in colonies. It has had many medicinal uses and is illegal to collect plants in the wild. Likes moist, rich woodlands.

Jacob's Ladder
Polemonium caeruleum

Late spring. Flowers are lavender-blue or white 1", cup-shaped, in clusters. Each flower has 5 rounded petals, 5 stamens with white anthers. The leaves are pinnately compound (leaflets are 1 - 2" long, oblong, opposite, thus resemble a ladder, referring to a ladder seen in a dream by the biblical Jacob). Leaf stems are 1 to 1-1/2' long and tend to arch and sprawl on the ground. Attracts butterflies and bees.

Pink Valerian
Valeriana pauciflora

Late spring. The pink or white cluster of funnel shaped flowers about 1/2" to 3/4" long at the top of the central stem has an appearance of fireworks going off in every direction. Tiny clusters of flowers may develop from the axils of the upper leaves. Also called Large Flowered Valerian, it is 1-1/2' to 3' tall, few if any, branches with a stout central stem. There are 3 leaflets per leaf on opposite sides of the stem. The leaflets are medium green, smooth, and slightly saw-tooth along their margins.

Waterleaf has 4 species:
1. Appendaged Waterleaf
Hydrophyllum appendiculatum

Late spring. Early spring leaves form a basal rosette, leaves almost twice as long as wide, with hairs barely noticeable and consisting of 5 - 7 lobes not divided completely to the mid-vein, have patches of greyish white water-stained appearance. A central stem emerges later and terminates in clusters of flowers. The basal leaves seem to rise up to become the lateral leaves when the flower stem emerges. So, if you see it in flower, you do not see the basal leaf clump that you might have seen earlier in the year. This biennial plant is 1 - 2' tall. This waterleaf has the most attractive flowers, usually lavender, about 1/2" - 3/4" across in the form of a corolla (petals are fused at the bottom) that consists of 5 petals, calyx with 5 narrow triangular teeth and 5 stamens. The flowers are above the leaves. Between each pair of teeth on the calyx, there is a short appendage that is strongly recurved. This reminds me of an aardvark face as in this photo. Alternate stem leaves have maple-like leaves that are up to 5" long and

wide divided into five lobes. It blooms for about 3 weeks and spreads by seeds.

Appendaged Waterleaf flower stem leaves.

2. Large Leaved Waterleaf
Hydrophyllum macrophylla

Very late perennial; in early spring leaves <u>form a basal rosette</u>, leaves nearly 3 times longer than wide with 9 or more deeply divided lobes on

Early basal leaves present before flowering.

the soft, hairy leaves. Later in spring it produces a stem with leaves longer than wide with about 5 lobes divided to near the middle, reaching to 1 - 2'. When the flowers appear you do not see the basal leaf clump that you might have seen earlier in the year. The flower stem terminates in a cluster of 8 - 20 blooms; 1/2" corollas in white, pink, or pale lavender with 5 petals, calyx with 5 teeth, and 5 stamens. It blooms later than Appendaged and is more likely to have white blooms.

3. Canada Waterleaf
Hydrophyllum canadense

Very late. Also known as **Bluntleaf, Broadleaf, and Mapleleaf Waterleaf.** Early spring leaves <u>do not form a basal rosette</u> but are found in colonies; length slightly more than width and the deep lobe divisions do not extend completely to the mid-vein; whitish water spots. Later in spring the leaves are about 18" tall, with a maple leaf shape. The flowers are below the leaves. The flower corolla is less than 1/2" long, 5-lobed, pink-white; 5 stamens extend beyond the corolla.

4. Virginia Waterleaf
Hydrophyllum virginianum

Late spring. Early leaves <u>do not form a basal rosette</u>, are slightly longer than wide with white spots; deeply divided to the middle vein. The stem has alternate leaves, 3 - 5 deeply divided lobes, narrow with acute tips. At the top is the cluster of 8 - 20 flowers which is 1" - 2" around. Each tiny flower is a 1/4" corolla with 5 lobes, calyx with 5 teeth, 5 stamens and 1 white style with a divided tip. The flowers are white, pink, or light lavender. The stamens extend far beyond the corolla.

Wild Hyacinth
Camassia scilloides

Late. A single stalk holds the terminal raceme of fragrant, white to light lavender flowers. Each flower, less than an inch, has 6 yellow anthers, and a green style. A raceme may hold up to 20 flowers. Also called camas, this spring-flowering bulb grows 1' - 2' tall. Grass-like leaves up to 12" long by 1/2" wide form the basal foliage. As an ephemeral, it fades away in summer. It is adaptable to a variety of growing conditions and tolerates clay soils.

Wild Geranium
Geranium maculatum

Late spring perennial, also called Crane's Bill. Rose-lilac flowers appear atop the foliage and are about 1" diameter with five petals and form clusters of 2 - 5 flowers for 6 - 7 weeks. It grows 1' - 2' tall with a cluster of opposite basal leaves containing five deep lobes, coarse teeth and 3" - 5" across. The plants spread using rhizomes and form colonies. Plants tolerate drier soils and partial sunlight.

Fleabanes
Erigeron spp.

Late spring daisy-like perennial or annual, is about 2' tall. It has slender stems with long, narrow elliptical, alternate leaves, from one to over 3" long and a basal clump of leaves. The flowers are small, only about a half inch diameter, emerging as a pale pink and opening to white petals and a yellow center disk. There are many species, some preferring open, sunny areas and others preferring moist, slightly shady locations. All are important for pollinators and wildlife forage. May form colonies with favorable growing conditions.

Guyandotte Beauty *Synandra hispidula*

A late spring biennial, this is an uncommon but strikingly beautiful white flower with pink stripes that reminds one of a Catalpa bloom, 3/4" to 1-1/2" long. It has opposite, heart-shaped leaves with serrated edges and stands at least 1' tall in moist, rich woods.

Yellow Violet
Viola pubescens

Mid-spring. A solitary yellow flower has five petals and usually grows singly rather than clusters. The pollen and nectar attract bees and butterflies. Preferring drier soil, this leafy stemmed violet grows 8 - 12" tall, has hairy, heart-shaped leaves with serrated edges.

Trout Lily, Yellow
Erythronium americanum

Mid-spring. Yellow flowers are 1-1/2" long, with 6 petals that curve upward in the daytime. This ephemeral occurs in dense colonies with thousands of leaves but much fewer blossoms. Plants can take up to seven years to flower from seed which accounts for fewer blossoms. Leaves are 4 - 6" long elliptical and mottled with brown splotches, resembling a trout fish.

Yellow Trillium
Trillium luteum

Mid-spring. Ephemeral up to 15" tall with three yellow petals atop three mottled leaves up to 4" long. Other uncommon yellow flowering trilliums are *Trillium recurvatum shayii* (Shay's Trillium) and *Trillium recurvatum lutescens*.

Large-Flowered Bellwort
Uvularia grandiflora

Mid-spring perennial 18 - 24" tall. The top of the plant tends to droop because of the weight of the leaves and flowers. The alternate leaves are elliptical, up to 6" x 2", smooth margins and parallel-veined. Each side stem terminates with a single yellow, six petal flower that has an elongated bell-like shape, 1 - 2" long. The plants' rhizomes form small colonies.

Yellow Corydalis
Corydalis flavula

Mid-spring. Tiny bright yellow flowers 1/2" long on a plant that is slender and wispy, up to 12" tall. The leaves resemble Dutchman's Breeches because both are deeply dissected and bloom around the same time. It likes rich soil in the open woods, usually on ridges and slopes in rocky areas.

Also called **Pale Corydalis, Yellow Harlequin,** and **Short-Spurred Corydalis.**

Pink Corydalis
Corydalis sempervirens

Late spring. Tiny bright yellow and pink flowers 1/2" long on a plant that is slender and dainty, up to 12" tall. The leaves resemble Dutchman's Breeches because both are deeply dissected and are close "cousins" in their classification

family. It likes rich soil in the open woods, and prefers sun but will sprout in a bit of shade. Foliage dies back in the heat of summer after seeds mature. When it is cool again in Autumn, the seeds sprout and the blue-green native is nearly evergreen in winter.

Marsh Marigold
Caltha palustris

Mid-spring. Bright yellow buttercup-like blossoms about 1/2" to 1-1/2" across with 5 to 9 petal-like sepals and occur in clusters. The shiny flowers appear over glossy, heart-shaped leaves on hollow, branching stems in a tight clump 1' to 1-1/2' tall. Attracts hummingbirds and butterflies. Always in wet soils near streams, marshes, wet meadows, or seeps.

INVASIVE Lesser Celandine or **Fig Buttercup**
Ficaria verna
(previously *Ranunculus ficaria*)

Blooming at the same time as dandelions and often confused with Marsh Marigold by the uninformed, is this **very invasive**, violet-sized, 3 - 9" tall plant that can quickly spread into a thick mat. Difficult to eradicate, as it has several tubers and bulblets when dug. Lesser Celandine is rarely near water and can consume entire woodlots. Native Marsh Marigold is a much larger plant that grows as a single clump in or near water.

Wood Poppy
Stylophorum diphyllum

A late spring ephemeral that has showy yellow 4 petal flowers, 1 - 2" across, and blooms for 3 - 4 weeks. Basal pairs of opposite leaves on a hairy stem, it reaches 12 - 18" in height with a stout rhizome. The leaves are deeply divided into five to seven irregular toothed segments and are green on top and grey underneath. The fruit is a grey, oval, hairy capsule that splits by longitudinal clefts into 3 to 4 segments.

INVASIVE   Greater Celandine
Chelidonium majus

Late spring. This **non-native invasive** plant originated in Europe and western Asia and is very similar to our native Wood Poppy. It is 1 - 2' tall and the flowers are only half the size of Wood Poppy, less than 1." Note the smooth, slender seed pods up to 2" long. It is listed as a noxious weed in some states and should not be moved or grown where it might escape.

Flower buds appear maroon, open petals are yellow.

Heart-Leaved Ragwort
Packera aurea

Late. Flowering stems are 1 - 2' tall. Clusters of yellow, daisy-like flowers 1" across sit on top. Stem leaves are sparse, finely cut, and oblong. Basal leaves are elongated heart-shaped with saw-toothed margins. The unopened flowers are maroon at the top of the stem. Also called **Golden Ragwort**, this weedy perennial is found in moist shady areas such as stream floodplains, wet woods, and ravines.

Round-Leaved Ragwort
Packera obovata

Late. Very similar to Heart-leafed Ragwort except that the flowers are smaller, about 3/4" across and the height of flowering stems are also smaller, up to 18." The basal leaves are round instead of the elongated heart shape. You will find it in shady areas with more drainage such as rocky hillsides, ledges, upper

stream banks, and moist flats. Both *Packera sp.* (aka. **Grounsel**) were previously *Senecio sp.* Other Ragworts: Prairie *(P. plattensis),* Balsam *(P. paupercula)* and Butterweed *(P. glabella).*

Swamp Buttercup
Ranunculus septentrionalis

Mid-spring. A small, 1" yellow, 5 - 8 petal flower on a short stem arises from a rosette of foliage near the ground. The 3" basal leaves are deeply divided into 3-parted dark green leaflets, which are deeply incised. It is an herbaceous perennial plant about 6" tall. Always found in soggy soil close to streams or seeps. It may cause skin   irritation.

Late winter-early spring   *later Spring*

Skunk cabbage   *Symplocarpus foetidus*

Very early. In late winter, foul-smelling maroon flowers, 3 - 5" tall, emerge from the ground before the leaves. The flower generates heat and can produce temperatures of 75 F, allowing them to melt snow. This warmth attracts early spring pollinators. Later, the leaves, which are about 8" x 12", emerge. This native is only found where the ground is consistently wet, on creek edges, or seeps. The large, cabbage-like plant grows in colonies and is ephemeral.

Early Meadow Rue
Thalictrum dioicum

Mid-spring. This plant grows up to 2' tall and has male and female flowers on separate plants. The male flowers are the most recognizable, 1/4" x 1/2" with dangling dull yellow tassels which are the anthers on the stamens.

The female flower is not noticeable, with no petals, and the same size as the male. The green leaves are compound with 3 - 12 lobes on a long, stalk.

The maroon tinted plant resembles Columbine.

Wild Ginger
Asarum canadense

Mid-spring. Large heart-shaped leaves are hairy, dark green, and deeply indented at the stem, grow in opposite pairs, with plant height about 8 - 10." The small maroon flower has 3 heart-shaped petals and is easily overlooked because they are near the base of the plant and hidden by the leaves. The flower is the color of decomposing flesh to attract small pollinating

flies that emerge from the ground early in the spring looking for a thawing carcass of an animal that did not survive the winter. It spreads easily in colonies.

Purple or Prairie Trillium
Trillium recurvatum

Mid-Late. A three-petal, maroon stalk-less flower, about 1" tall, has 3 sepals pointing down (recurved). Three leaves are on top of an 8 - 12" stem, usually a mottled green, and are 3 - 5" long. These ephemerals form colonies, spreading by rhizomes. Similar in appearance to the Sessile Trillium.

**Sessile Trillium
or Toad-shade**
Trillium sessile

Mid-Late. This ephemeral is only 5 - 8" tall. The flower has three maroon petals, 1" tall and three sepals on top of the leaves. Three mottled leaves are just 2 - 3" long at the top of the stem. Sessile means "without a stalk" and that applies to leaves and flowers. Similar to Purple Trillium with small anatomical differences.

Red Trillium
Trillium erectum

Mid-Late ephemeral. A three-petal maroon flower is held above the leaves and sits on top of an ascending nodding peduncle 1½ - 3" long. The plant is 1 - 2' tall, has 3 sepals and 3 mottled green leaves which are 3 - 8" long. Seed takes 5 - 10 years to flower. The root system is rhizomatous, eventually forming colonies.

Fire Pink *Silene virginica*

A clump-forming perennial with fuzzy, sticky stems 12 - 20" tall. It is native to rocky wooded slopes, and prefers some sun. This plant has

bright scarlet flowers 2" across with five petals notched at the tip forming a five pointed star shape. Sepals form a long sticky tube. Flowers bloom April to June on top of slender stems with lance shaped, green leaves up to 1-1/4" x 6" or more. Basal leaves 3/4" x 4" are oblong to spatula shaped.

Jack-in-the-Pulpit

Arisaema triphyllum

This is the maroon color pattern of Jack-in-the-Pulpit. See previous entry on page 45.

Late summer red fleshy coated seeds

Wild Columbine
Aquilegia canadensis

Late. Each flower is about 1-1/2" long and hangs down from a long stalk, having 5 petals and stamens. Each petal is yellow and rounded toward the tip, but its base consists of a long nectar spur that is a pale red to maroon. Sparingly branched, it gets 1 - 3' tall. At first, only basal leaves are produced, but later leaves emerge along the stems divided into groups of three. Each leaflet is up to 2 x 3" and divides into 3 rounded lobes also having secondary lobes.

Dwarf Larkspur
Delphinium tricorne

Mid-spring. 1 - 2' tall herbaceous plants with alternate 4" leaves deeply divided into 5 - 7 separate lobes. A raceme of flowers about 4"-8" long sit at the top of each stalk. Each dark, blue-violet flower is about 3/4" to 1" across, consisting of 5 petal-like sepals, 4 petals, 3 inner pistils, and stamens. As a member of the delphinium family, Greek for dolphin, that refers to the flower shape. The flowers attract bees and hummingbirds.

Common Blue Violet
Viola sororia

Mid-spring. Light blue to violet flowers are 3/4"
across and have 5 rounded petals; 2 upper
petals, 2 side petals with white hairs (beards)
near the throat, and a lower petal that is a
landing pad for insects. Each flower rests on top
of a leafless stalk. The heart-shaped basal
leaves are slightly serrated and up to 3" x 3."
This vigorous, rhizomatous, low-growing
perennial is only 3 - 8" tall. It is an adaptable
ground cover for areas along walkways or
under shrubs.

Alphabetical Index by Common Name

Notes:

_____

_____

_____

_____

_____

_____

_____

_____

_____

_____

_____

References and More Information:
(more than one reference used for each entry)

Websites:
http://www.missouribotanicalgarden.org/plantfinder/
    plantfindersearch.aspx
https://www.illinoiswildflowers.info
https://www.nps.gov/ National Park Service
https://www.fs.usda.gov/ USDA Forest Service
https://gobotany.nativeplanttrust.org

Reference Books:
Wildflowers and Ferns of Indiana Forests
    by Michael A. Homoya, 2012.
Wildflowers Northeastern/Northcentral North
    America by Roger Tory Peterson & Margaret
    McKenny, 1968.

Notes:

_____

_____

_____

_____

_____

_____

_____

About the Author: Tess Park, DVM graduated from Purdue University College of Veterinary Medicine in 1977 where she learned about wildflowers in Toxicology class. After graduation, she and her husband, Jay, purchased a 3.3 acre property in 1978, where they still live in Indiana. Although there has

been a home on the property since 1905 and previous owners had farm animals, the one acre of woods still had many wildflowers. They began to identify them and add more to their collection. They also love to hike and photograph wildflowers as well as identify trees along the way. They have been caretakers of their land and avid plant collectors and members of plant societies. Their son, John, also enjoys the outdoors.